Contents

How to use this book — 2

21a Rounding — 3–6

21b Multiplication and division — 7–10

22a Subtraction — 11–14

22b Subtraction — 15–18

23a Subtraction — 19–22

23b Multiplication — 23–26

24a Weight — 27–30

24b Co-ordinates — 31–34

25a Direction — 35–37

25b Angle — 38–41

26a Multiplication and division — 42–45

26b Multiplication — 46–49

27a Multiplication — 50–53

27b Division — 54–57

28a Fractions — 58–61

28b Fractions and decimals — 62–65

29a Addition — 66–69

29b Subtraction — 70–73

30a Time — 74–77

30b Data — 78–80

How to use this book

Each page has a title telling you what it is about.

Instructions look like this. Always read these carefully before starting.

This shows you how to set out your work. The first question is done for you.

Read these word problems very carefully. Decide how you will work out the answers.

This is Owl. Ask your teacher if you need to do his questions.

These are exploratory activities. You may want to discuss them with a partner.

Rounding

The rabbits are having a hopping contest.

Write each distance hopped to the nearest 10 cm.

1.⬚8⬚0⬚cm

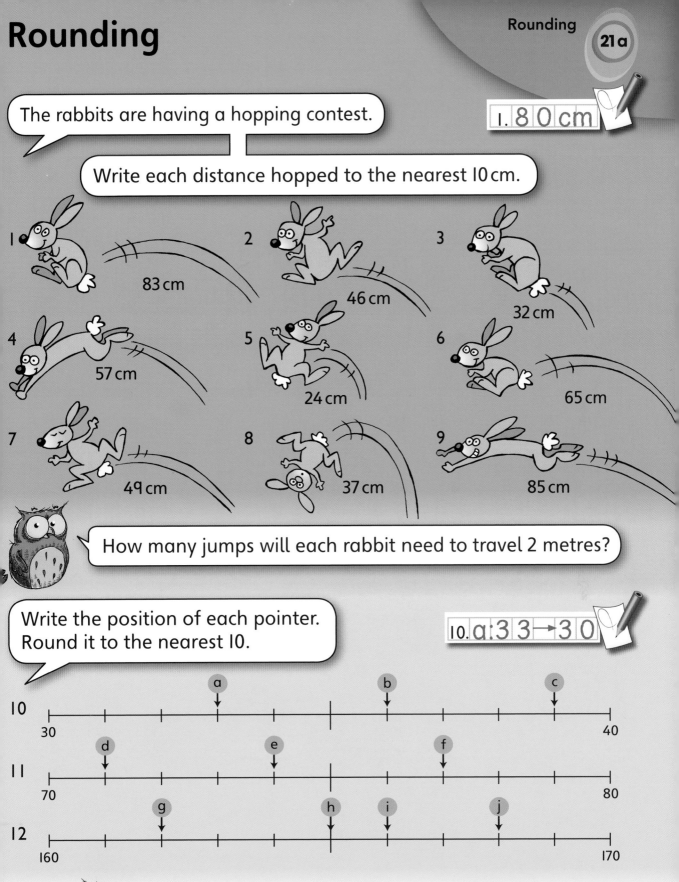

1   83 cm

2   46 cm

3   32 cm

4   57 cm

5   24 cm

6   65 cm

7   49 cm

8   37 cm

9   85 cm

How many jumps will each rabbit need to travel 2 metres?

Write the position of each pointer.
Round it to the nearest 10.

10. a:⬚3⬚3⃗⬚3⬚0

10   a   b   c
    30   40

11   d   e   f
    70   80

12   g   h   i   j
    160   170

Write all the numbers that could
round to 40 as the nearest 10.

3

Rounding

Write each weight, then round it to the nearest 100 g.

1. 360 g   400 g

Is the total weight of all six rabbits more or less than 2 kg? By how much?

Round the weights of these rabbits to the nearest (a) 100 g (b) 10 g.

5. (a) 236 g → 200 g
   (b) 236 g → 240 g

5   236 g

6   347 g

7   188 g

8   425 g

9   634 g

10   857 g

A rabbit's weight has been rounded to 700 g to the nearest 100 g. What could his weight be? His sister's weight is rounded to 520 g to the nearest 10 g. What could her weight be?

Rounding

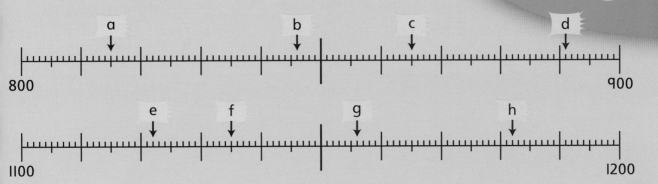

Write the position of the flags whose numbers round to:

1.c:865, ...

1   900 to the nearest 100

2   820 to the nearest 10

3   1160 to the nearest 10

4   1100 to the nearest 100

5   850 to the nearest 10

6   1120 to the nearest 10

For each calculation, choose the closest approximation.

7.200+40

7   $196 + 43$ —————→

| 190 + 40 | 200 + 40 |
| 200 + 10 | 190 + 50 |

8   $378 - 162$ —————→

| 370 − 160 | 400 − 160 |
| 380 − 200 | 380 − 160 |

9   $58 × 471$ —————→

| 50 × 400 | 50 × 470 |
| 60 × 500 | 60 × 470 |

10 $886 ÷ 27$ —————→

| 880 ÷ 30 | 900 ÷ 30 |
| 890 ÷ 20 | 890 ÷ 30 |

11 $£5·26 + £18·39$ —————→

| £5 + £18 | £5 + £19 |
| £6 + £18 | £6 + £19 |

Write some calculations for which 230 + 70 is a good approximation.

Rounding

Round each amount to the nearest (a) £1 (b) 10p.

1. (a) £3·87 → £4
   (b) £3·87 → £3·90

1	£3·87	2	£4·65
3	£9·86	4	£4·93
5	£5·46	6	£7·38
7	£6·08	8	£11·44
9	£31·64	10	£48·59

How many 2p coins will match each rounded amount?

11 Mr Green rounds all his prices to the nearest 10p. If he sells one of each item, will he be better off with rounded or unrounded prices? How about 10 of everything?

£1·46

£1·21

£3·67

£2·32

94p

£2·97

Having rounded the prices, which items should he sell lots of to be better off?

Multiplying by 10 and 100

Each hedgehog does a sponsored walk around their gardens. Write how far each walks after 10 laps of the garden.

1

I lap = 45 m

2

I lap = 38 m

3

I lap = 62 m

4

I lap = 74 m

5

I lap = 28 m

6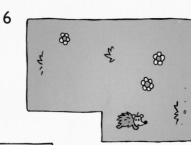

I lap = 104 m

7

I lap = 96 m

8

I lap = 65 m

9

I lap = 19 m

Write how far after 100 laps of the garden.

 If the hedgehogs are sponsored £5 per kilometre, which ones earn more than £20 after 100 laps?

Copy and complete.

$$10.\ 35 \times 10 = 350$$

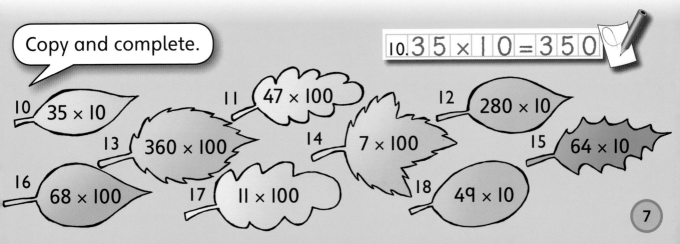

10 35×10

11 47×100

12 280×10

13 360×100

14 7×100

15 64×10

16 68×100

17 11×100

18 49×10

Dividing by 10 and 100

Write the number of pounds by dividing by 10 or 100.

1. $4800 \div 100 = £48$

1
4800
1p coins

2
750
10p coins

3
6400
1p coins

4
800
1p coins

5
4600
10p coins

6
770
10p coins

7
690
10p coins

8
9800
10p coins

9
7400
1p coins

Your aunt offers you either 10p a day for a year or £3 a month for a year. Which is better?

Copy and complete.

10. $840 \div 10 = 84$

10 $840 \div 10$

11 $5600 \div 100$

12 $7600 \div 10$

13 $7900 \div 100$

14 $48\,000 \div 100$

15 $85\,000 \div 100$

16 $950 \div 10$

17 $480 \div 10$

18 $8000 \div 10$

Multiplying and dividing by 5 and 20

I. $10 \times 43p = 430p$
   $= £4·30$

Write the cost of:

1   10 Cheese   2   10 Chicken   3   10 Onion

Cheese 43p 	Onion 51p 	Traditional 38p
Lamb and mint 32p	Chicken 65p 	Sweet potato 48p

---

Multiply by 10, then use doubling and halving to find the cost of:

4   20 Traditional   5   20 Sweet potato   6   5 Lamb and mint

---

True or false?

7   To multiply by 100, multiply by 10 and then by 10 again.

8   To divide by 20, divide by 10 and then double it.

9   To multiply by 5, multiply by 10 and then halve it.

10 To divide by 5, divide by 10 and then halve it.

A bag contains 2000 coins.   **Write how much is in the bag if they are all:**

11 1p coins   12 10p coins   13 £2 coins

14 2p coins   15 50p coins   16 20p coins

Multiplying and dividing

1 Naresh collects 20p coins.
He has saved £7·80.
How many coins is this?

2 Sally gets £5 pocket money
every week. How much does
this cost her parents every year?

Explore

Invent a rule for these, starting by multiplying by 10 and 100:

3 Multiplying by 50

4 Multiplying by 200

5 Multiplying by 11

6 Multiplying by 9

Try the rules on these numbers: 43   18   160

Copy and complete.

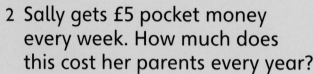

7. $73 \times 10 = 730$

7 $73 \times 10 = \boxed{}$

8 $42 \times 100 = \boxed{}$

9 $3900 \div 100 = \boxed{}$

10 $860 \times 10 = \boxed{}$

11 $47 \times 5 = \boxed{}$

12 $960 \div 20 = \boxed{}$

13 $28 \times 50 = \boxed{}$

14 $8600 \div 200 = \boxed{}$

15 $32 \times 200 = \boxed{}$

16 $3800 \div 50 = \boxed{}$

Subtracting

How much has been cut off each plank?

1.
3 6 3	3 7 0		4 0 0	
	↘7↗ +	↘3 0↗	= 3 7	cm

1
363 cm

Was 4 metres

2
126 cm

Was 2 metres

3
284 cm

Was 3 metres

4
378 cm

Was 4 metres

5
436 cm

Was 5 metres

6
152 cm

Was 2 metres

 Write two numbers whose difference is 99. Repeat. What patterns can you see?

Write how much each snake grows.

7.
1 2 7	1 3 0		1 9 2	
	↘3↗ +	↘6 2↗	= 6 5	cm

7 started at 127 cm
reaches 192 cm

8 started at 235 cm
reaches 281 cm

9 started at 128 cm
reaches 182 cm

10 started at 216 cm
reaches 274 cm

11 started at 368 cm
reaches 391 cm

12 started at 136 cm
reaches 205 cm

Subtracting

How much longer is one ladder than the other?

1. $362 - 178 = 184$ cm

$$178 \quad 180 \quad 200 \quad 362$$
$$\searrow 2 + \searrow 20 + \searrow 162 = 184$$

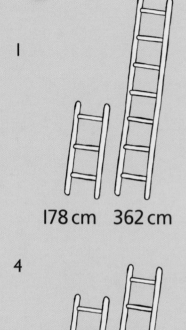

1

178 cm   362 cm

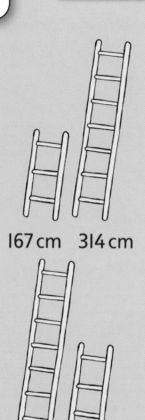

2

167 cm   314 cm

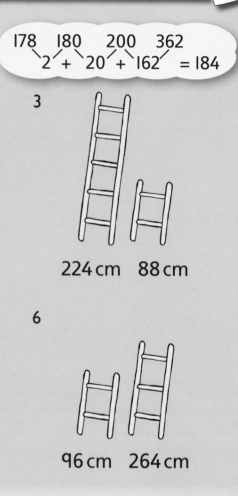

3

224 cm   88 cm

4

176 cm   241 cm

5

341 cm   142 cm

6

96 cm   264 cm

7 Anjilee has saved £316 towards a holiday costing £600. How much more must she save? If insurance costing £58 is added, how much does she need now?

8 Nick climbs 214 feet up a cliff. The top is 512 feet above the sea. He started at 28 feet above sea level. How far has he yet to climb? How far will he climb in total?

Write a 3-digit number using next-door numbers, e.g. 543. Reverse the digits to make a new number (345). Find the difference. Repeat this. What patterns can you see?

Subtracting

How much further has the top climber in each pair risen?

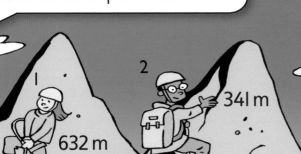

```
1.   200
     632
    -375
           5 → 380
          20 → 400
         232 → 632
         257 m
```

1 632 m
375 m

2 341 m
154 m

3 418 m
242 m

4 527 m
314 m

5 492 m
356 m

6 397 m
123 m

Copy and complete.

7   325 − 187 =

8   162 − 88 =

9   243 − 168 =

10 525 − 377 =

11 613 − 366 =

12 457 − 239 =

Write pairs of heights where the difference is a 3-digit number with next-door digits, e.g. 123, 234; 345 …

13

Subtracting

Choose a pair of numbers. Work out the difference. Repeat this to find all ten pairs.

Estimate first

1.
```
     400
     712
  -  345
       5 → 350
      50 → 400
     312 → 712
     367
```

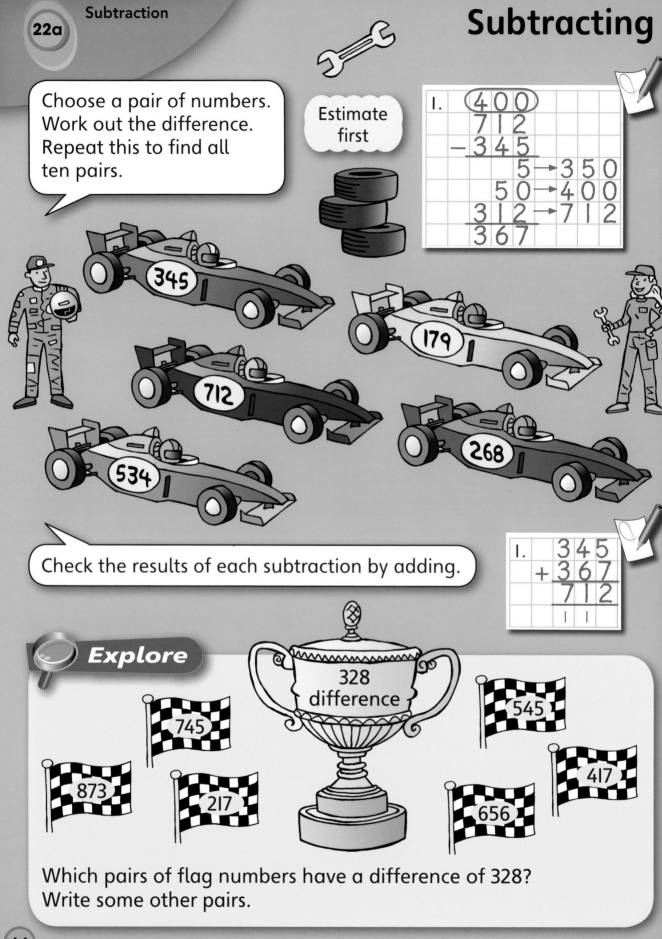

345

179

712

268

534

Check the results of each subtraction by adding.

1.
```
     345
  + 367
     712
     1 1
```

Explore

328 difference

745

545

873

217

656

417

Which pairs of flag numbers have a difference of 328?
Write some other pairs.

Subtracting

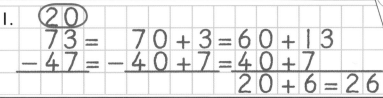

Copy and complete.

1.
$$73 = 70 + 3 = 60 + 13$$
$$-47 = -40 + 7 = 40 + 7$$
$$20 + 6 = 26$$

1   73 − 47 =

2   61 − 43 =

3   82 − 58 =

4   71 − 38 =

5   62 − 27 =

6   74 − 46 =

7   65 − 18 =

8   53 − 26 =

Write two numbers whose difference is equal to the smaller number. Do this six times. What do you notice?

9

Choose two numbers.

Subtract the smaller from the larger.

Do this six times.

74

65

38

57

82

Subtracting

Subtract 333 from each number.

1.
$$426 = 300 + 120 + 6$$
$$-333 = -300 + 30 + 3$$
$$90 + 3 = 93$$

(100)

| 1 | 426 | 2 | 541 | 3 | 628 | 4 | 417 | 5 | 522 | 6 | 642 |

Now subtract 251 from each number.

7 Sean had collected 121 football cards. He gave Jason 68. How many did he have left?

8 The train travelled 328 miles on its journey. The last 162 miles were without heating! For how many miles was the heating on?

9 Sarita weighed out 320 g of butter. When she turned her back, the cat ate 178 g. How much was left?

10 Ling had a satin ribbon that was 226 cm long. She cut off 152 cm. What length did she have left? How much less than half is that?

Guess how many times you can subtract 121 from 1000. Now work it out with your partner.

Subtracting

Copy and complete.

(270)

$346 = 300 + 40 + 6 = 200 + 140 + 6$
$-84 = -\quad\quad 80 + 4 = -\quad\quad 80 + 4$
$\quad\quad\quad\quad\quad\quad\quad\quad\quad\quad 200 + 60 + 2 = 262$

1
346
− 84

2
248
− 73

3
126
− 62

4
482
− 76

5
335
− 82

6
137
− 85

7
227
− 64

8
124
− 86

Choose a subtraction you found hard. With a partner, add the answer to the smaller number to check it.

How much further to read?

9

 146

261 pages in total

10

158

372 pages in total

11

165

481 pages in total

12

137

564 pages in total

13

128

473 pages in total

14

147

583 pages in total

Use number cards 1–9.
Make a subtraction like this:

□ □ □
− □ □ □

Complete the subtraction. Check by adding.

Subtracting

Copy and complete.

1. 200

	2	4	1
	3	5	4
−	1	6	7
	1	8	7

1   354
   − 167

2   423
   − 176

3   524
   − 178

4   325
   − 158

5   436
   − 187

6   341
   − 174

This is Tim's homework. He got some subtractions wrong. Where did he make the errors?

7   4 ²3̷ ¹7
    − 1 2 9
      3 0 8

8   2 ⁷8̷ ¹4
    − 1 3 9
      1 4 4

9   ³4̷ ¹⁰0̷ ¹6
    − 1 8 3
      2 2 7

10   ⁵6̷ ³3̷ ¹9
    − 2 5 4
      3 8 5

11   5 2 4
    − 1 8 3
      4 1 1

12   ²3̷ ¹³4̷ ¹1
    − 1 5 8
      1 8 3

Use these cards:

| 1 | 3 | 4 | 5 | 7 | 8 |

Make a subtraction like this:

Find ways that give the largest answer, the smallest answer, and the answer closest to 100.

Subtracting

How many centimetres must each giraffe stretch?

383 \ 390 / 400
\7/ + \10/
400 − 383 = 17 cm

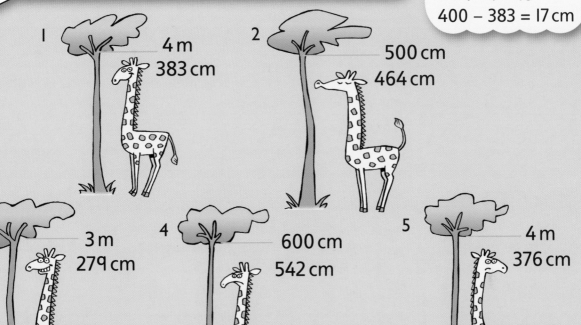

1 4 m 383 cm

2 500 cm 464 cm

3 3 m 279 cm

4 600 cm 542 cm

5 4 m 376 cm

 Invent a giraffe question for your friend. Write the height of the giraffe and the height of the leaf it has to reach.

How much must be added to get a multiple of 1000?

6. 4997 + 3 = 5000

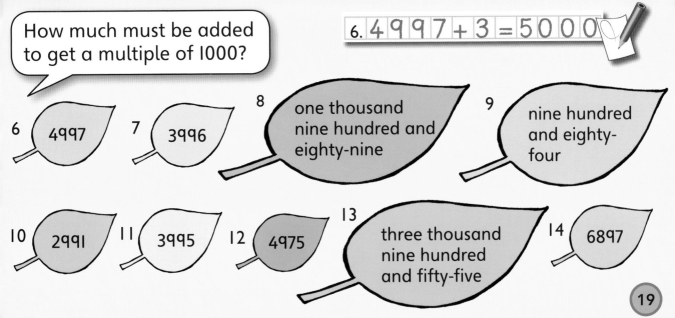

6 4997

7 3996

8 one thousand nine hundred and eighty-nine

9 nine hundred and eighty-four

10 2991

11 3995

12 4975

13 three thousand nine hundred and fifty-five

14 6897

19

Subtracting

Complete the subtractions, using the number lines to help you.

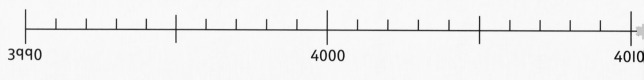

1. 4 0 0 3 − 3 9 9 6 = 7

3990   4000   4010

1   4003 − 3996   2   4009 − 3991

6990   7000   7010

3   7006 − 6997   4   7005 − 6994

5   7008 − 6993   6   7011 − 6994

How many subtractions are there crossing 1000 where the difference is 10?

7   Choose two aeroplanes.   Write the difference in the distances travelled.   Repeat six times.

6043 miles

5025 miles

5985 miles

4998 miles

3970 miles

Subtracting

Write the difference between the crowd today and the crowd last Saturday.

1. 5014 − 4973 = 41

1

today: 5014
last Saturday: 4973

2

today: 3028
last Saturday: 2947

3

today: 3987
last Saturday: 4017

4

today: 5020
last Saturday: 4991

5

today: 2996
last Saturday: 3051

6

today: 2079
last Saturday: 1981

Every spectator bought a 25p programme. Choose a match and work out how much more money would be taken on the busier Saturday.

7 Tom the builder bought 5000 staples to fix the tiles on the roof. He used 4892. How many did he have left?

8 In one savings account Mr Rich had £4017. In another he had £3925. How much more did he have in the first account?

9 One aeroplane flew 4036 miles and a second one flew 3975 miles. How much further did the first plane fly?

Subtracting

Write the difference between the two amounts.

1. £1046 – £989 = £57

1. £1046   £989

2. £5054   £4973

3. £3024   £2994

4. £4069   £3876

5. £2055   £1988

6. £4078   £3942

7. £1098   £976

8. £6038   £5984

9. £4036   £3828

10. £5095   £4865

11. £3069   £2876

12. £2067   £1978

Explore

Beth and Juan have £5000 in £5 notes. They share it unequally. Beth complains that Juan has £80 more. How many notes do they each have?

Nines

Use fingers to help you answer each question.

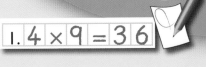 1. $4 \times 9 = 36$

1

$4 \times 9 = \square$

4   $3 \times 9 = \square$

7   $10 \times 9 = \square$

2

$5 \times 9 = \square$

5   $8 \times 9 = \square$

8   $2 \times 9 = \square$

3

$9 \times 9 = \square$

6   $7 \times 9 = \square$

9   $6 \times 9 = \square$

Planet stickers come in packs of 9.
How many packs are there in each box?

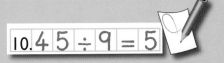 10. $45 \div 9 = 5$

10

45 stickers

11

63 stickers

12

27 stickers

13

81 stickers

Write the digits 0–9 in order. Write the digits 0–9 in reverse order underneath.

    ... 8, 9

    ... 1, 0

Read the numbers vertically. What do you notice?

Nines

Each cat has nine lives.
How many lives in each set?

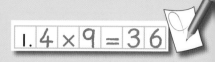

1. $4 \times 9 = 36$

1

2

3

4

5

6

7

8

9

Copy and complete.

10 $1 \times 9 =$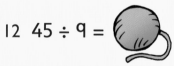

11 $6 \times 9 =$

12 $45 \div 9 =$

13 $3 \times 9 =$

14 $5 \times 9 =$

15 $54 \div 9 =$

16 $4 \times 9 =$

17 $63 \div 9 =$

18 $9 \times 9 =$

Nines

Write out the ×9 table. Use it to help you complete each number sentence.

1 ☐ × 9 = 18

2 3 × 9 = ☐

3 72 ÷ 9 = ☐

4 ☐ ÷ 9 = 10

5 4 × 9 = ☐

6 9 × ☐ = 9

7 ☐ ÷ 9 = 9

8 ☐ ÷ 5 = 9

9 ☐ × 9 = 72

10 54 ÷ ☐ = 9

11 ☐ × 9 = 63

12 36 ÷ ☐ = 9

True or false?

13 In a multiplication fact where one number is 9, the answer has digits that add up to 9.

14 Three nines is an even number.

16 If an even number is multiplied by 9 the answer is always odd.

15 When a number is multiplied by 9, the answer is always odd.

18 If an odd number is multiplied by 9 the answer is always even.

17 Seven nines is a number that ends in 9.

Write your own statement about the ×9 table. Is it true or false? Ask your partner to say which.

Nines

Write the position of each pointer.

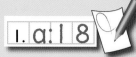
1
a   b

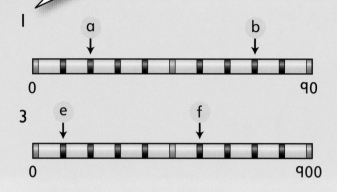

0   90

2
c   d

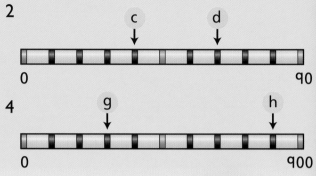

0   90

3
e   f

0   900

4
g   h

0   900

5   Pandit paid 9p for every sticker. He has 9 stickers. How much did he spend?

6   A dressmaker sewed 9 sequins onto each dress. She had 72 sequins. How many dresses did she decorate?

7   Cans of drink are sold in packs of 9. Dad bought 6 packs and his children drank 5 each day. How long did the packs last?

🔍 Explore

Take a number, for example: 549

Add the digits: $5 + 4 + 9 = 18$

Add the digits of the answer.
Keep going until you reach a single digit: $1 + 8 = 9$

If the digit is 9, it means that the number is in the ×9 table.

Write ten numbers greater than 500 that are in the ×9 table.

Weight

> What unit would you use to measure the weight of each creature?

1. spider: grams

1
2
3
4
5
6
7

> Write each amount in grams.

8. 1 kg = 1 0 0 0 g

8 1 kg

9 $\frac{1}{2}$ kg

10 $\frac{1}{4}$ kg

11 $1\frac{1}{2}$ kg

12 $\frac{3}{4}$ kg

13 $1\frac{1}{4}$ kg

14 2 kg

15 $1\frac{3}{4}$ kg

16 $2\frac{1}{4}$ kg

> Think of an animal. Discuss with your partner what unit you would use to weigh it. Repeat for a different animal.

Weight

Write the most likely weight of each creature.

1. mouse: 200g

1

10g   200g   2kg

2

1kg   2g   20g

3

8kg   20kg   20g

4

2g   10kg   100kg

5

3g   700g   10kg

6

1g   1kg   2kg

Take off your shoes! Feel their weight. Write an estimate in grams. Use scales to weigh them. How close was your estimate?

Write each amount in kilograms.

7. 1250g = 1¼ kg

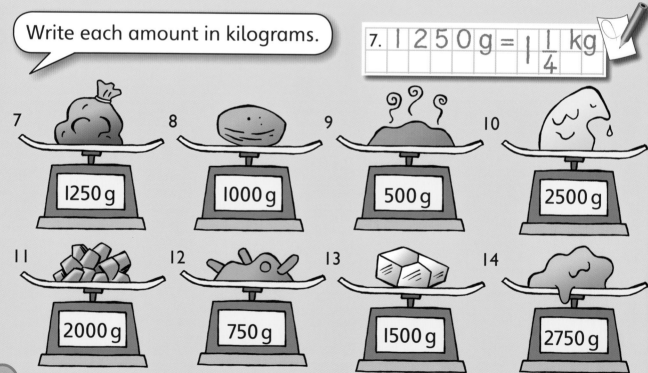

7 1250g

8 1000g

9 500g

10 2500g

11 2000g

12 750g

13 1500g

14 2750g

Weight

Write the weight of the food in grams.

1. 5 0 0 g

1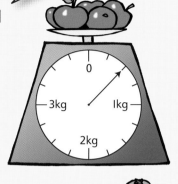

2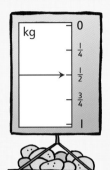

3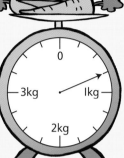

4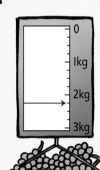

5

6

Write the weight of 10 times each amount in kilograms.

True or false?

7   1 kg is more than 500 g.

8   $1\frac{3}{4}$ kg is the same as 1750 g.

9   Two $\frac{1}{2}$ kg bags of coal are heavier than a 1 kg bag of cotton wool.

10 Three $\frac{1}{2}$ kg packets of flour weigh exactly 1600 g.

11 Five 200 g weights are the same weight as 1 kg.

12 A hamster could weigh 50 kg.

Write your own statement about weight. Ask your partner if it is true or false.

Weight

Choose parcels to match the weights on each scale.

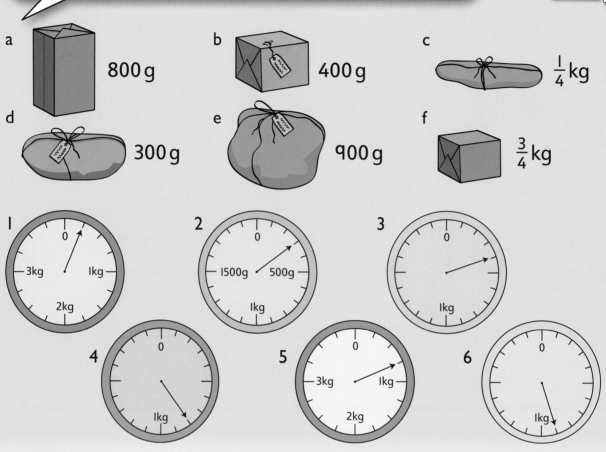

a 800 g

b 400 g

c $\frac{1}{4}$ kg

d 300 g

e 900 g

f $\frac{3}{4}$ kg

1   0   3kg   1kg   2kg

2   0   1500g   500g   1kg

3   0   1kg

4   0   1kg

5   0   3kg   1kg   2kg

6   0   1kg

It costs 25p per 100 g to send a parcel.
How much will it cost to send each parcel?

7   Kim has a bag weighing 20 kg and one half that weight. She loses a 300 g book. How much weight is she carrying?

8   Tim soaked 100 g of rice in water. It doubled in weight. To have $\frac{1}{2}$ kg of soaked rice, how much more soaked rice must Tim add?

9   Shelly has $\frac{1}{2}$ kg of corn. She eats 200 g. How much does she have left? If she gives 200 g to her brother, how much is left now?

Co-ordinates

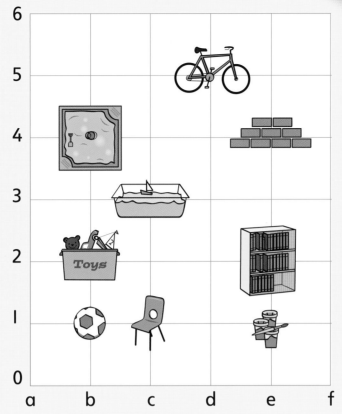

Write the co-ordinates of each object.

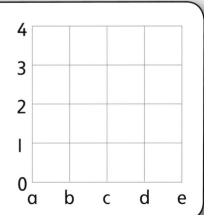

1. football (b, 1)

1	football	2	chair	3	bookshelves
4	bike	5	sand tray	6	bricks
7	water tray	8	toy box	9	paints

Draw a small 4 × 4 grid. Number the vertical side and put letters along the bottom.
Draw things on the grid and write their co-ordinates.

Co-ordinates

What objects are at the following co-ordinates?

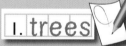
1. trees

1 (b, 2)	2 (e, 1)	3 (h, 4)
4 (e, 5)	5 (b, 4)	6 (b, 5)
7 (h, 6)	8 (d, 3)	9 (h, 1)

Look at a street map of your local area.
How are the lines or spaces labelled?

Co-ordinates

Write the co-ordinates for each place.

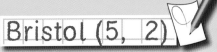

Bristol (5, 2)

For which places on the map is the first co-ordinate more than the second co-ordinate?

33

Co-ordinates

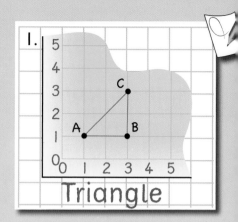

1.
Triangle

Draw a 10 × 10 grid.

Number the lines horizontally and vertically.

Mark each set of co-ordinates and join the points to make a shape.

Write the name of the shape.

1 A   B   C
   (1, 1) (3, 1) (3,3)

2 D   E   F   G
   (4, 1) (4, 3) (6, 1) (6, 3)

3 H   I   J   K
   (7, 3) (7, 6) (9, 3) (9, 6)

4 L   M   N
   (4, 4) (6, 4) (5, 6)

5 O   P   Q   R   S   T   U   V
   (2, 5) (3, 5) (4, 6) (4, 7) (3, 8) (2, 8) (1, 7) (1, 6)

 Explore

This point has co-ordinates that add to 10. Plot other points that do the same. What is the pattern? Plot co-ordinates that add to 6.

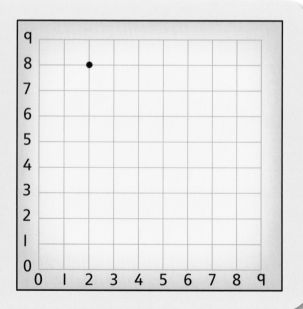

Direction

 is North. Write the direction of the arrows.

1

2

3

4

5

6

7

8

Write some pairs of directions that are opposite each other, e.g. North and South.

Where do you get to if you go:

9. Riptide

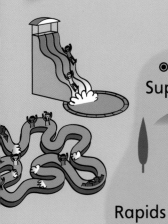

Super Slide

 Riptide

Deluge

Surf Central

Rapids

Log Flume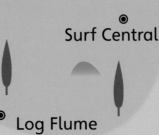

9 East from Super Slide

10 South from Riptide

11 West from Surf Central

12 North from Rapids

13 North-east from Log Flume

14 South-west from Deluge?

Follow the directions.
Which city do you reach?

1. Tokyo

1   South from Akita

2   South-west from Osaka

3   North-east from Matsue

4   North-west from Osaka

5   East from Hiroshima

6   West from Tokyo

7   South-west from Hiroshima

8   East from Matsue

9   Bristol is north-east of Exeter. What direction is Exeter from Bristol?

10 Manchester is west of Sheffield and Birmingham is south of Sheffield. What is the direction of Manchester from Birmingham?

11 Bristol is west of London and Cardiff is west of Bristol. Milford Haven is west of Cardiff. In which direction should I travel to go from Milford Haven to London?

Direction

Write the direction to go from one city to the other.

1. South-east

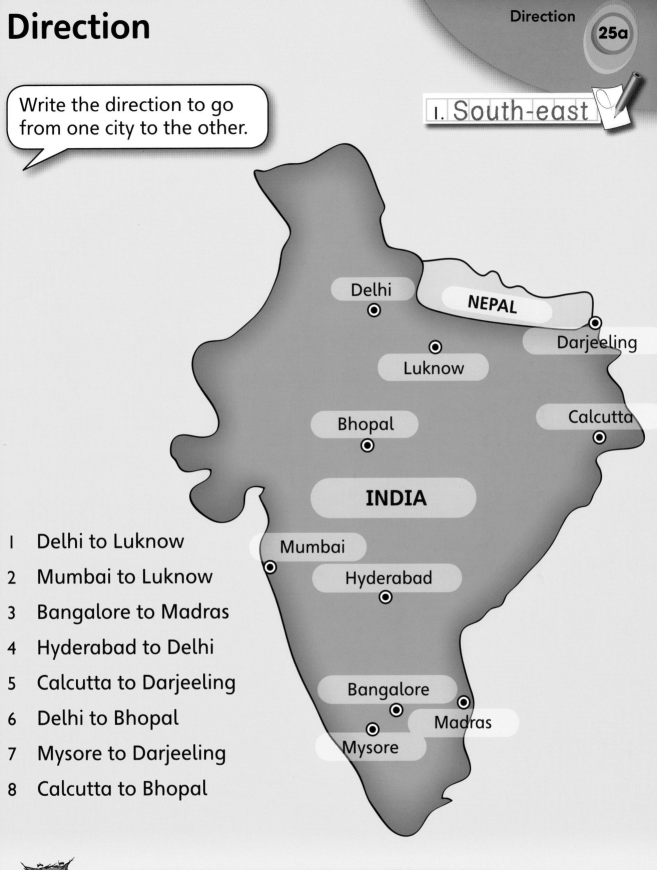

Delhi

NEPAL

Darjeeling

Luknow

Bhopal

Calcutta

INDIA

Mumbai

Hyderabad

Bangalore

Madras

Mysore

1 Delhi to Luknow

2 Mumbai to Luknow

3 Bangalore to Madras

4 Hyderabad to Delhi

5 Calcutta to Darjeeling

6 Delhi to Bhopal

7 Mysore to Darjeeling

8 Calcutta to Bhopal

Look for a map of India in an atlas.
Write some direction questions of your own.

Angles

How many right angles?

1. 2 right angles

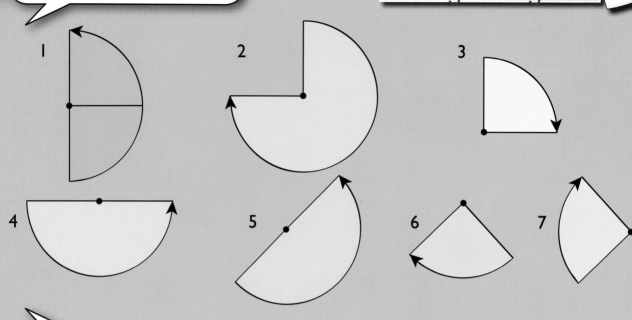

1

2

3

4

5

6

7

Write the number of degrees in each angle.

If the compass needle turns clockwise, how many right angles does it turn through?

8. 2 right angles

8   Starts pointing East, ends pointing West

9   Starts North, ends South

10 Starts South, ends East

11 Starts East, ends South

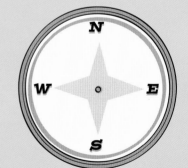

If the needle turns anti-clockwise, how many right angles?

Work with a partner. Draw a line on some squared paper. They draw a line at right angles to it. You draw a line at right angles to their line. Keep going to make a pattern.

Angles

All these turns are clockwise. Write the direction of each plane after they turn.

1. South

1 flying North

turns 180°

2 flying East

turns 90°

3 flying north-west

turns 90°

4 flying south-east

turns 180°

5 flying West

turns 90°

6 flying north-east

turns 90°

How many degrees?

7. 180°

7

8

9

10

Start with a compass face. How many different ways can you shade a right-angle turn?

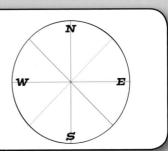

39

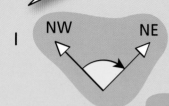

Angles

Write the number of degrees.

1. 90°

1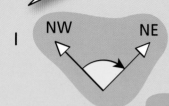

2

3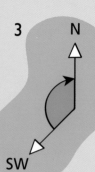

4

5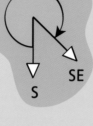

6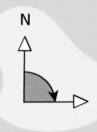

7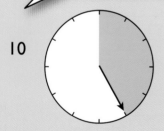

8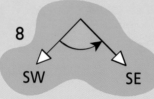

9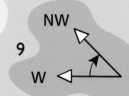

Draw different changes of direction for a 90° turn. How many can you find?

Write the number of degrees.

10. 90°+60°=150°

10

11

12

13

14

15

Angles

Write the angle in degrees turned by the minute hand. 1. 90°

1

2

3

4

5

6

7

8

9

10

 Explore

Explore how many right angles the hour hand of your clock turns in one day. Try it for the minute hand.

Sevens

Write how many days old these puppies are.

1

4 weeks

2

5 weeks

3

7 weeks

4

3 weeks

5

6 weeks

6

2 weeks

7

9 weeks

8

8 weeks

9

11 weeks

If a puppy becomes a dog after 42 weeks, for how many days is it a puppy?

Copy and complete.

10. $5 \times 7 = 35$

10 $5 \times 7 = $

11 $10 \times 7 = $

12 $2 \times 7 = $

13 $7 \times 7 = $

14 $3 \times 7 = $

15 $6 \times 7 = $

16 $4 \times 7 = $

17 $9 \times 7 = $

18 $11 \times 7 = $

19 $8 \times 7 = $

20 $0 \times 7 = $

21 $20 \times 7 = $

Sevens

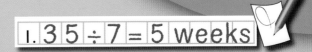

1. $35 \div 7 = 5$ weeks

Lucy is counting the days in her diary. Write how many weeks until each event.

1. 35 days before going camping

2. 21 days to her birthday

3. 56 days to the concert

4. 14 days to Clare's wedding

5. 63 days to the summer holiday

6. 49 days to the end of term

7. 28 days before going to Waterworld

8. 42 days to the school trip

9. 77 days to Mum's birthday

 Find out how many days to some events of your own. Write them as weeks.

Copy and complete.

10. $21 \div 7 = 3$

10. $21 \div 7 = $
11. $70 \div 7 = $
12. $14 \div 7 = $
13. $28 \div 7 = $
14. $49 \div 7 = $
15. $42 \div 7 = $
16. $7 \div 7 = $
17. $35 \div 7 = $
18. $77 \div 7 = $
19. $63 \div 7 = $
20. $56 \div 7 = $
21. $700 \div 7 = $

Sevens

Snow White goes shopping for the seven dwarves. She buys these for each of them. Write how many of each she needs to buy.

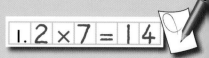
1. 2 × 7 = 14

1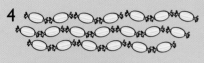

2

3

4

5

6

7

8

9

If Snow White gave each dwarf one sweet every day, what is the most sweets she will need to buy for any month?

These apples come in bags of seven, one for each day of the week.

Write how many bags you would need to have one apple every day for:

10 28 days

11 63 days

12 77 days

13 140 days

14 half a year

15 5 years

Sevens

Copy this table.

2s	2	4	6	8	10					
5s	5	10	15							
7s	7	14								
10s										

1 Complete the 2s and 5s.

2 Find the 7s by adding the 2s and 5s.

3 Find the 10s.

4 Find the 7s by subtracting the 3s from the 10s.

Use the 7s to write the ×14 multiplication table.

I am a multiple of 7. Who am I in each question?

5 Both my digits are odd. I am less than 70.

6 My digit total is a multiple of 10.

7 One of my digits is double the other. I am also a multiple of 3.

Write the missing values.

8. $3 \times 7 = 21$

8 $3 \times 7 = $ 🌸

9 ✴ $\div 7 = 2$

10 🌼 $\times 7 = 42$

11 🌼 $\div 7 = 3$

12 $28 \div 7 = $ 🌼

13 🌸 $\times 7 = 63$

14 🌼 $\times 7 = 49$

15 $42 \div 7 = $ 🌸

16 🌼 $\div 7 = 5$

17 🌸 $\times 7 = 56$

18 $5 \times 7 = $ 🌼

19 🌸 $\div 7 = 8$

Multiplying

New-Look windows are in the shape of regular polygons. Write the perimeter of each.

$1. 4 \times 20 = 80 \, cm$

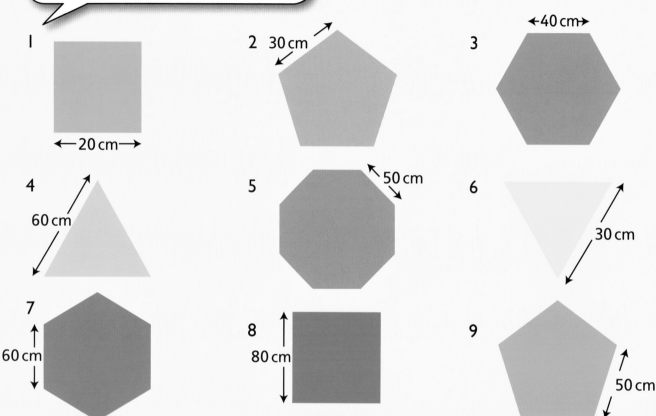

1 ←20 cm→

2 30 cm

3 ←40 cm→

4 60 cm

5 50 cm

6 30 cm

7 60 cm

8 80 cm

9 50 cm

One of the windows has a perimeter of 480 cm. What shape could it be and what is its side length?

Write an estimate of the perimeters of these regular polygons by rounding.

$10. 5 \times 50 = \ldots \, cm$

10 pentagon, side 48 cm

11 hexagon, side 33 cm

12 square, side 62 cm

13 triangle, side 37 cm

14 octagon, side 59 cm

15 heptagon, side 72 cm

Multiplying

> Copy and complete.

1 $3 \times 43 = (3 \times 40) + (3 \times 3) = 120 + 9 = $

2 $4 \times 36 = (4 \times 30) + (4 \times 6) = \quad + \quad = $

3 $5 \times 27 = (5 \times 20) + (5 \times 7) = \quad + \quad = $

4 $9 \times 17 = (9 \times \quad) + (9 \times \quad) = \quad + \quad = $

5 $7 \times 52 = (7 \times \quad) + (7 \times \quad) = \quad + \quad = $

6 $6 \times 24 = (\quad \times \quad) + (\quad \times \quad) = \quad + \quad = $

7 $8 \times 32 = (\quad \times \quad) + (\quad \times \quad) = \quad + \quad = $

> Write the cost of these jacket potatoes.

8. $3 \times 32 = (3 \times 30) + (3 \times 2)$
   $= 90 + 6$
   $= 96p$

8   3 with beans

9   4 with sweetcorn

10 6 with tuna

11 5 with mushy peas

12 7 with chilli

13 8 with coleslaw

14 3 with sweetcorn and 4 with beans

15 4 with tuna and 3 with chilli

Beans 32p	Coleslaw 35p
Sweetcorn 28p	Tuna 57p
Mushy peas 42p	Chilli 46p

> If four people order one jacket potato each, what could the total cost be?

Multiplying

Copy and complete these multiplication grids. Write a multiplication for each.

1.
	30	7
5	150	35

150
+ 35
185

$5 \times 37 = 185$

1
	30	7
5		

2
	40	3
6		

3
	20	8
3		

4
	70	2
4		

5
	30	4
8		

6
	40	2
9		

Complete these multiplications. Estimate first, then draw a grid.

7. estimate: $3 \times 30 = 90$
	20	7
3	60	21

$3 \times 27 = 81$

7 3×27

8 4×43

9 5×38

10 6×74

11 7×33

12 8×29

Can you find a multiplication like this that has an answer near to 236?

Multiplying

1　Ian bought 4 apples at 23p each and 3 oranges at 32p each. How much change did he have from £5?

2　The bus fare to work is 24p each way. What is the cost for a 5-day week? How much cheaper is a travel pass, costing £1·85 a week?

3　Tickets for the match cost £34 for adults and £18 for children. What is the cost for a family of 4 adults and 3 children?

Find how to arrange the digits like this: ☐ × ☐☐ to make these answers.

4　4　3　5 ⟶ 215

5　6　7　2 ⟶ 182

6　8　4　6 ⟶ 288

7　2　5　8 ⟶ 140

8　4　3　7 ⟶ 148

9　9　7　8 ⟶ 632

Use number cards 2–9.

Choose three to make a multiplication like this: ☐☐ × ☐

Explore how many different answers you can make between 100 and 300.

Multiplying

Copy and complete these multiplications. Estimate first.

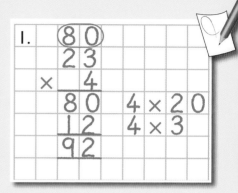

1.
```
   80
   23
×   4
   80   4 × 20
   12   4 × 3
   92
```

1 ⟨80⟩
   23
 × 4

       4 × 20
       4 × 3
   ——

   ——

2 ⟨280⟩
   42
 × 7

       7 × 40
       7 × 2
   ——

   ——

3   38
   × 3

4   82
   × 6

5   28
   × 5

6   56
   × 4

7   63
   × 6

How many days has each child been at school?

8

16 weeks

9

23 weeks

10

35 weeks

11

43 weeks

12

19 weeks

13

28 weeks

How many days have you had at school this term? How about last term?

Multiplying

Gabby makes phone calls to her friends in different countries:

Shelley
26p per minute

Simon
14p per minute

Azize
34p per minute

Lizzie
18p per minute

Sangeet
24p per minute

Zoe
37p per minute

Write the cost of a call to:

1. Shelley for 6 minutes

2. Sangeet for 3 minutes

3. Lizzie for 9 minutes

4. Zoe for 4 minutes

5. Azize for 5 minutes

6. Simon for 7 minutes

```
1.    1 5 0
         2 6
      ×     6
      1 2 0
         3 6
      1 5 6 p
      = £ 1·56
```

Write the cost of an 8-minute call to each friend.

Gabby has only £2 left for one phone call. For how many minutes could she talk to each friend?

7. 80 children are told to sit in 3 rows of 24. How many will have to stand?

8. The school canteen arranges the buns in rows of 4 buns. Each tray can hold 23 rows. How many buns can 3 trays hold?

Multiplying

Complete these multiplications.

Estimate first.

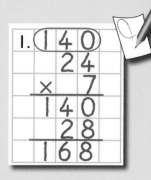

1.
```
  (1 4 0)
      2 4
  ×     7
  1 4 0
    2 8
  1 6 8
```

1 24
   × 7

2 43
   × 8

3 27
   × 5

4 36
   × 6

5 84
   × 3

6 28
   × 9

7 72
   × 4

8 85
   × 7

9 48
   × 3

 **Peckles** 32p *Yummy for birds!*

 **Tasty Pex** 63p *Birds love 'em!*

 **Beakstoppers** 18p

 **BREKSEEDS** 27p

 **LUSH Berries** 48p

 **Cheese Worms** 10 worms for 17p

Write the cost of:

10 6 packets of Lush Berries

11 4 bags of Brekseeds

12 7 packets of Peckles

13 5 packets of Tasty Pex

14 8 Beakstoppers

15 40 Cheese Worms

You have £5 to spend on a treat for your bird. What will you choose?

Multiplying

violin
£86

horn
£28

drum
£32

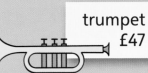
trumpet
£47

flute
£43

cymbals
£24

cello
£63

clarinet
£58

saxophone
£74

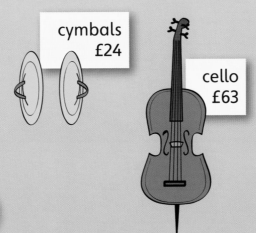

Write the cost of:

1   six violins

2   three drums

3   four trumpets

4   two flutes

5   six clarinets

6   three cellos

7   seven saxophones

8   four horns

9   two cymbals

```
1. £ 5 4 0
       8 6
   ×     6
     4 8 0
       3 6
   £ 5 1 6
```

Explore

Use these cards: 3 4 5 6

Arrange three of them like this: ☐ ☐ × ☐

Explore the largest and smallest possible answers.

Do the same with these cards: 6 7 8 9

Dividing

Copy and complete these divisions.

1
$4\overline{)48}$
_____ 10×4
_____ 2×4

2
$6\overline{)78}$
_____ 10×6
_____ 3×6

3
$5\overline{)85}$
_____ ☐ $\times 5$
_____ ☐ $\times 5$

4
$3\overline{)51}$
_____ ☐ $\times 3$
_____ ☐ $\times 3$

5
$8\overline{)96}$
_____ ☐ $\times 8$
_____ ☐ $\times 8$

Each freezer is packed with ready meals.
Cara needs to eat 3 meals a day.
For how many days could Cara survive?

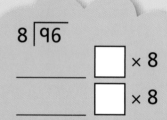

6.	3	4	8
	1	6	

6

48 ready meals

7

54 ready meals

8

57 ready meals

For each freezer, how many days could
Big Colin survive eating 4 meals a day?

Dividing

How many days will it take to finish each book?

1. $4\overline{)72}$
   40   10×4
   ... 8×4

1

72 pages
4 pages a day

2

51 pages
3 pages a day

3

75 pages
5 pages a day

4

84 pages
6 pages a day

5

96 pages
4 pages a day

6

84 pages
3 pages a day

How long will it take to read all six books by reading 10 pages a day?

Copy and complete these divisions.

7 $3\overline{)45}$ 8 $5\overline{)95}$ 9 $3\overline{)54}$

10 $4\overline{)76}$ 11 $6\overline{)72}$ 12 $5\overline{)65}$

13 $4\overline{)68}$ 14 $7\overline{)84}$ 15 $3\overline{)75}$

Dividing

Each group played in the concert.

Their earnings are shared among the group members.

How much did each musician earn?

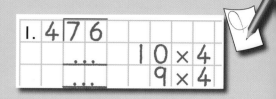

1.
4	7	6		
		...	10×4	
		...	9×4	

1 The Four Multiples
£76

2 The Clockwise Three
£51

3 The Polygons
£85

4 The Two Co-ordinates
£88

5 The Four Right Angles
£92

6 The Fraction Boyz
£96

All the groups earned the same, and each musician's share is a whole number of pounds. What could they have earned?

Write the cost of each concert ticket.

7.
3	5	4

7 Total:
£54

8 Total:
£92

9 Total:
£65

10 Total:
£91

11 Total:
£96

12 Total:
£69

Dividing

> Each group shares the sweets.

> How many do they get?
> Are there any left over?

```
1.      15 r 2
     3 ) 47
        30      10 × 3
        17
        15       5 × 3
         2
```

1

47 sweets

2

82 sweets

3

59 sweets

4

73 sweets

5

57 sweets

6

83 sweets

7

75 sweets

8

45 sweets

Explore

Choose a number between 5 and 10. Which numbers between 60 and 100 give a remainder of 1 when divided by your number? Which give a remainder of 2? of 3?

9 Ling has 72 stickers, and can put 4 on each page in her album. How many pages can she fill?

10 Three friends go out for dinner, and the bill comes to £81. They share the bill and give a tip of £2·50 each. How much does each pay?

11 90 footballers arrive for a 5-a-side competition. How many teams can be made, and how many matches can be played in the first round?

Fractions of amounts

Write the fractions of the stamps.

Use the lines to help you.

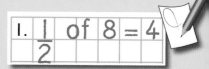
1. $\frac{1}{2}$ of 8 = 4

1

$\frac{1}{2}$ of 8 = ☐ $\frac{1}{4}$ of 8 = ☐

2

$\frac{1}{2}$ of 12 = ☐ $\frac{1}{3}$ of 12 = ☐ $\frac{1}{6}$ of 12 = ☐

3

$\frac{1}{2}$ of 10 = ☐ $\frac{1}{5}$ of 10 = ☐

4

$\frac{1}{2}$ of 18 = ☐ $\frac{1}{3}$ of 18 = ☐ $\frac{1}{6}$ of 18 = ☐

Complete the fractions of the coins.

Use 1p coins to help you.

5

$\frac{1}{3}$ of ☐ p = ☐ p

6

$\frac{1}{4}$ of ☐ p = ☐ p

7 $\frac{1}{2}$ of 10p = ☐

8 $\frac{1}{4}$ of 20p = ☐

9 $\frac{1}{3}$ of 12p = ☐

10 $\frac{1}{5}$ of 15p = ☐

11 $\frac{1}{2}$ of 14p = ☐

12 $\frac{1}{4}$ of 16p = ☐

How many 1p coins do you need to be able to split a set into halves, thirds, quarters and fifths?

Fractions of amounts

Write the fractions of red cubes.

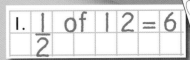

1. $\frac{1}{2}$ of 12 = 6

1

2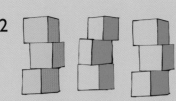

3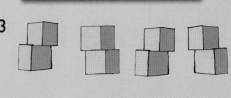

4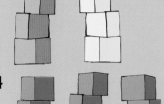

5

6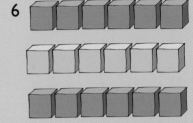

7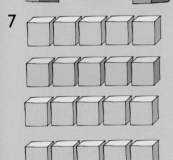

8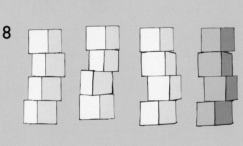

9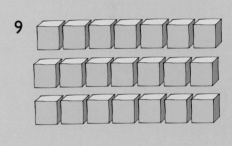

 $\frac{1}{4}$ of a pile of cubes is 2 more than $\frac{1}{5}$ of the same pile. How many cubes are there? Suppose it was 4 more?

Copy and complete.

10. $\frac{1}{2}$ of 14 = 7

10 $\frac{1}{2}$ of 14 = ☐

11 $\frac{1}{3}$ of 21 = ☐

12 $\frac{1}{4}$ of 20 = ☐

13 $\frac{1}{5}$ of 45 = ☐

14 $\frac{1}{6}$ of 30 = ☐

15 $\frac{1}{3}$ of 18 = ☐

16 $\frac{1}{10}$ of 70 = ☐

17 $\frac{1}{8}$ of 48 = ☐

18 $\frac{1}{7}$ of 49 = ☐

19 $\frac{1}{6}$ of 42 = ☐

20 $\frac{1}{9}$ of 72 = ☐

21 $\frac{1}{4}$ of 32 = ☐

Fractions of amounts

1   In a class of 32, $\frac{1}{4}$ are absent. Of those present, $\frac{1}{3}$ are boys. How many girls are present?

2   Snappy the crocodile was born with 40 teeth. He lost $\frac{1}{5}$ of his teeth in his first year, and another $\frac{1}{4}$ of those left in the next year. How many teeth does he have left now?

3   Sarita bought a tin of 60 fruit gums. She kept $\frac{1}{3}$ for herself, gave $\frac{1}{4}$ to her sister and $\frac{1}{5}$ to her brother. How many are left for her Mum and Dad?

Write the difference between:

4   $\frac{1}{4}$ of 12 and $\frac{1}{3}$ of 15

5   $\frac{1}{7}$ of 42 and $\frac{1}{4}$ of 36

6   $\frac{1}{5}$ of 45 and $\frac{1}{4}$ of 40

7   $\frac{1}{10}$ of 90 and $\frac{1}{8}$ of 56

8   $\frac{1}{6}$ of 72 and $\frac{1}{3}$ of 54

9   $\frac{1}{5}$ of 100 and $\frac{1}{4}$ of 100

Look at the differences you have written. If the difference between two fractions of amounts is 5, what could they be?

Explore

Use between 15 and 25 counters.

$\frac{1}{4}$ of 20 = 5

Make as many different fractions of the counters as you can and write them down.

$\frac{1}{3}$ of 21 = 7

Fractions of amounts

Copy and complete.

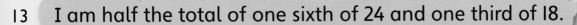

1. $\frac{1}{3}$ of 9 = 3 → $\frac{2}{3}$ of 9 = 6

1 $\frac{1}{3}$ of 9 = ☐ ⟶ $\frac{2}{3}$ of 9 = ☐

2 $\frac{1}{4}$ of 12 = ☐ ⟶ $\frac{3}{4}$ of 12 = ☐

3 $\frac{1}{5}$ of 20 = ☐ ⟶ $\frac{4}{5}$ of 20 = ☐

4 $\frac{1}{6}$ of 42 = ☐ ⟶ $\frac{5}{6}$ of 42 = ☐

5 $\frac{1}{10}$ of 60 = ☐ ⟶ $\frac{7}{10}$ of 60 = ☐

6 $\frac{1}{8}$ of 64 = ☐ ⟶ $\frac{3}{8}$ of 64 = ☐

7 $\frac{3}{5}$ of 15 = ☐   8 $\frac{3}{4}$ of 28 = ☐   9 $\frac{7}{10}$ of 80 = ☐

I am a number. Who am I?

10   I am one half of a fifth of 20.

11   I am 3 less than double one third of 21.

12   I am 5 more than a fifth of double 20.

13   I am half the total of one sixth of 24 and one third of 18.

14   I am the difference between one quarter of 60 and one fifth of 60.

15   I am the total of one half, one third and one quarter of 24.

Invent your own 'Who am I?' problems using fractions, with the answers. Try them on a friend.

Write the fraction of the coloured part of each square.

1 |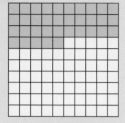
2 |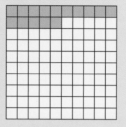
3 |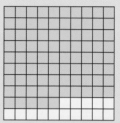

4 |
5 |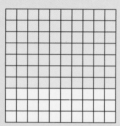
6 |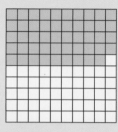

7 |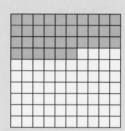
8 |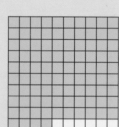
9 |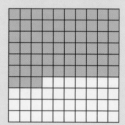

Write each coloured fraction as a decimal.

Write each fraction as a number of hundredths.

Use a 10 × 10 square to help you.

10 one half　　11 one quarter　　12 one tenth

13 three quarters　　14 seven tenths　　15 one fifth

Seven tenths lies between 50 and 80 hundredths. Can you find some other fractions that lie between this number of hundredths?

Hundredths

Write the value of each underlined digit.

1. <u>3</u> tenths

| 1 | 1·3<u>4</u> | 2 | 2·5<u>6</u> | 3 | <u>3</u>7·82 | 4 | 4·0<u>8</u> | 5 | 13·<u>7</u>2 | 6 | 28·4<u>7</u> |

Write some decimal numbers between 5 and 10 where the digits have a total of 12, e.g. 6·33.

Write the position of each pointer as a decimal.

7. (a) 3·2

7

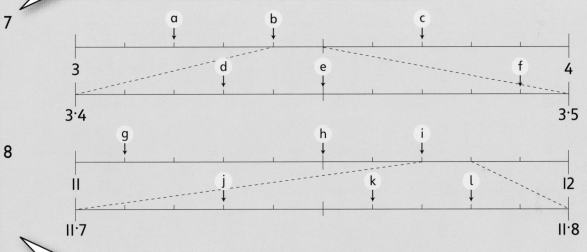

8

Write the position of each pointer as a mixed number.

7. (a) $3 \frac{2}{10}$

Write as decimals:

9. 2·35

| 9 | $\frac{235}{100}$ | 10 | $\frac{140}{100}$ | 11 | $\frac{657}{100}$ | 12 | $\frac{480}{100}$ |

Write as mixed numbers:

| 13 | 0·96 | 14 | 2·45 | 15 | 7·31 | 16 | 5·08 |

Hundredths

Write the amount in each pile.

1. £6·59

1

2

3

4

5

6

7

Write the amounts in order, smallest to largest.

If you took 10 coins from a mixed bag of lots of £1, 10p and 1p coins, what amounts could you have?

Write the letter to match each of these positions on the lines:

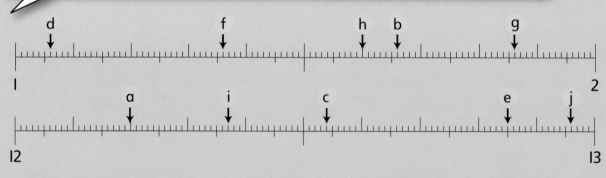

8 1·66   9 12·2   10 1·36   11 12·54   12 1·6

13 12·85   14 1·06   15 12·96   16 1·86   17 12·37

How many decimal numbers between 1·5 and 2·12 have 1 as their hundredths digit? 2 as their hundredths digit?

Hundredths

Write the heights of the stilt-walkers in metres.

1. 2·8 5 m

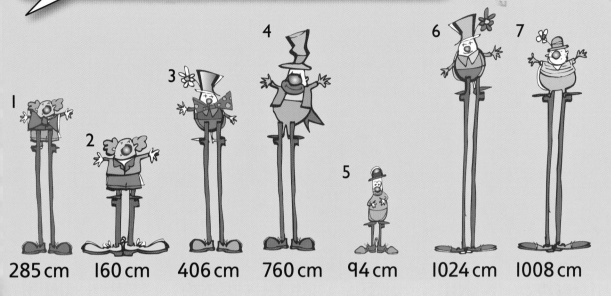

285 cm   160 cm   406 cm   760 cm   94 cm   1024 cm   1008 cm

About how many metres taller than you are each of these stilt-walkers?

Copy and complete.

8   80 hundredths = tenths

9   17 tenths = hundredths

10 320 hundredths = tenths

11 100 tenths = hundredths

Write the number that is exactly half way between:

12. 4·5

12 4 and 5

13 4·4 and 5

14 4·4 and 4·5

15 4·41 and 4·49

16 4·42 and $4\frac{1}{2}$

17 $4\frac{44}{100}$ and 4·48

18 $4\frac{1}{4}$ and $4\frac{45}{100}$

19 4·04 and 4·4

Adding money

£5·50 is added to the cost of each ticket. Write the total to pay. Estimate first!

1.
```
  £ 2 1
  £ 1 6 · 2 7
+ £   5 · 5 0
  £ 2 1 · 7 7
        1
```

1 AMSTERDAM £16·27

2 BRISTOL TICKET £8·25

3 TICKET EXETER £4·35

4 PARIS £25·19

5 DUBLIN flight £12·49

6 MADRID £32·35

7 ROME £27·20

Which pairs of tickets can be bought with £30?

Copy and complete.

8.
```
  £ 7
  £ 3 · 8 4
+ £ 2 · 7 5
  £ 6 · 5 9
        1
```

8
```
  £3·84
+ £2·75
```

9
```
  £4·75
+ £1·72
```

10
```
  £3·27
+ £2·38
```

11 £2·83 + £1·34

12 £5·25 + £2·37

13 £4·61 + £3·96

14 £6·34 + £1·57

15 £3·84 + £2·74

16 £5·66 + £2·52

Adding money

1

> Choose two books. Work out the total cost. Repeat six times.

1.
```
  £ 1 1
  £ 5·6 4
+ £ 4·8 9
  £10·5 3
     1 1
```

ROBIN HOOD
£5·64

DINOSAUR WORLD
£4·89

FOOTBALL
£7·71

HORSE
£6·58

WIZARDS ADVENTURE
£7·65

ART & CRAFT BOOK
£8·93

> What numbers could you use to make this addition work? Write your own question for a friend to answer. Make sure you can solve it yourself!

```
  £ 4 · ☐ 6
+ £ ☐ · 5 ☐
  £ 1 0 · 0 0
```

> Copy and complete. Write an estimate first.

8.
```
  £ 1 1
  £ 3·3 2
  £ 4·5 3
+ £ 3·4 5
  £11·3 0
     1 1
```

2   £3·32 + £4·53 + £3·45

3   £4·36 + £2·27 + £2·15

4   £2·81 + £1·91 + £1·73

5   £3·21 + £2·32 + £3·97

6   £4·14 + £3·67 + £2·15

7   £4·53 + £2·62 + £1·41

Adding money

Copy and complete. Write an estimate first.

1.
```
   £7
   £2·75
 + £3·86
   £6·61
     1 1
```

1   £2·75 + £3·86

2   £3·66 + £7·75

3   £4·84 + £8·96

4   £3·47 + £2·86

5   £4·57 + £1·68

6   £2·75 + £2·49

7   £5·48 + £1·75

8   £4·87 + £1·56

9   Choose three videos.   Estimate first, then find the total cost.   Repeat six times.

£7·75

£5·69

£8·66

9.
```
   £23
   £7·75
   £5·69
 + £8·66
   £22·10
     2 2 2
```

£6·77

£8·94

£7·86

Use a calculator to find the cost of all the videos.

 Invent some different prices of three DVDs that have a total of exactly £15.

Adding money

1 Choose two amounts to make each total. Write each addition.

Amounts

£3·68 £4·75 £5·69 £5·86 £6·57 £5·38

Totals

£12·43 £9·06 £10·44 £8·43 £11·24 £12·26

2 Raj saved £7·95. He won a raffle prize of £12·55 and then found £2·37 in his pocket. How much has he got in total?

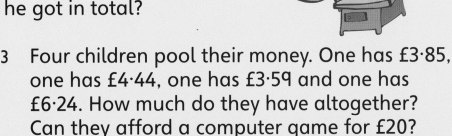

3 Four children pool their money. One has £3·85, one has £4·44, one has £3·59 and one has £6·24. How much do they have altogether? Can they afford a computer game for £20?

4 There are four tickets left for a football match. One costs £8·56. the second costs 10p more, the third costs 20p more and the fourth costs 30p more. How much do they cost in total?

5 The roller coaster is £1·93, the slide is £1·54, the roundabout is 86p, the dodgems are £2·67 and the freefall is £3·38. How much does it cost to go on all the rides?

Write two amounts that add to make £10. The two amounts must have completely different digits and both must have digits in the £, 10p and 1p columns.

Subtracting money

Reduce each price by £1·30. Estimate first.

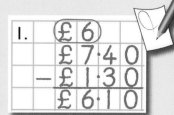

	£	6		
1.	£	7	4	0
−	£	1	3	0
	£	6	1	0

1  £7·40

2  £8·40

3  £9·60

4 £7·70 LOST IN SPACE

5  SONIC THE MOUSE £8·90

6  FORMULA ONE £6·80

7  £5·70 FLIGHT DECK

Estimate how many times you can subtract £1·60 from the most expensive computer game. Do the subtraction to see how close you were.

Copy and complete. Estimate first.

	£	2		
8.	£	4	5	2
−	£	2	3	6
	£	2	1	6

8   £4·52
    − £2·36

9   £2·73
    − £1·48

10 £3·42 − £1·28

11 £4·66 − £2·48

12 £6·72 − £3·16

13 £5·53 − £3·27

14 £4·61 − £2·48

15 £5·88 − £4·69

Subtracting money

£4·42

£3·84

£5·53

£6·61

1.
```
  £ 4
  £⁷8·²6
− £ 4·4 2
  £ 3·8 4
```

Help each child choose a T-shirt. Estimate how much money they will have left, then work it out.

1 £8·26

2 £9·18

3 £10·37

4 £5·28

5 £10·38

6 £9·29

7 £7·36

8 £8·28

9 £10·17

Find the difference. Estimate first.

10.
```
  £ 1
  £³4·¹1 9
− £ 3·2 6
  £ 0·9 3
```

10 £4·19   £3·26

11 £4·75   £8·26

12 £4·57   £2·86

13 £5·48   £2·75

14 £6·94   £1·26

15 £5·86   £3·47

16 £4·38   £1·64

17 £7·72   £2·19

Invent a subtraction with an answer of £2·36. Give it to your partner to try.

71

Subtracting money

How much more is one pair of sunglasses than the other? Estimate first.

1.
$$\begin{array}{r} £1 \\ £2\overset{13}{\cancel{4}}{}^{1}8 \\ -£1\cdot69 \\ \hline £0\cdot79 \end{array}$$

1   £1·69   £2·48

2   £3·12   £1·87

3   £3·24   £1·76

4   £5·16   £2·87

5   £2·43   £1·95

6   £2·32   £2·65

7   Gemma bought a lipstick for £5·50, and an eyeliner for £3·75. How much was the eye shadow if she spent £10·20 in total?

8   Tariq bought a computer game for £15·20. He is now selling it for £7·75. He wants to buy another game for £9·26. How much more does he need?

9   Two pairs of trainers cost £28·25 and £21·66. How much do you save if you buy one expensive pair rather than two cheaper pairs?

Copy and complete.   Estimate first.

10   £3·23 – £1·88

11   £14·14 – £9·85

12   £9·23 – £5·76

13   £12·40 – £4·97

14   £8·12 – £4·86

15   £5·21 – £3·75

Use the digits 1, 2, 3, 7, 8 and 9 to make two amounts where the difference is £6·43.

Subtracting money

Give Ruth's homework a mark out of 9.
Point out any mistakes you find!

1
$$\begin{array}{r} \overset{3}{\cancel{4}}\overset{1}{\cdot}28 \\ -1\cdot73 \\ \hline 2\cdot55 \end{array}$$

2
$$\begin{array}{r} \overset{4}{\cancel{5}}\cdot\overset{1}{4}6 \\ -2\cdot75 \\ \hline 2\cdot71 \end{array}$$

3
$$\begin{array}{r} \overset{7}{\cancel{8}}\cdot\overset{1}{3}9 \\ -1\cdot64 \\ \hline 6\cdot75 \end{array}$$

4
$$\begin{array}{r} 8\cdot\overset{8}{\cancel{9}}\overset{1}{1} \\ -1\cdot08 \\ \hline 7\cdot13 \end{array}$$

5
$$\begin{array}{r} \overset{5}{\cancel{6}}\cdot\overset{12}{\cancel{3}}\overset{1}{5} \\ -2\cdot48 \\ \hline 3\cdot87 \end{array}$$

6
$$\begin{array}{r} \overset{8}{\cancel{9}}\cdot\overset{12}{\cancel{3}}\overset{1}{5} \\ -8\cdot67 \\ \hline 0\cdot68 \end{array}$$

7
$$\begin{array}{r} 14\cdot\overset{2}{\cancel{3}}\overset{1}{6} \\ -7\cdot29 \\ \hline 7\cdot07 \end{array}$$

8
$$\begin{array}{r} 15\cdot\overset{6}{\cancel{7}}\overset{1}{1} \\ -9\cdot08 \\ \hline 6\cdot64 \end{array}$$

9
$$\begin{array}{r} 2\overset{0}{\cancel{1}}\cdot\overset{12}{\cancel{3}}\overset{1}{0} \\ -6\cdot75 \\ \hline 14\cdot55 \end{array}$$

 Explore

Choose two amounts.

Find the total.
Find the difference.

Subtract one answer from the other.

Double the smaller of the two original amounts and repeat,
using this and your answer from the subtraction.

What do you notice? Repeat with two different amounts.

£6·82   £2·75   £5·54

£2·36   £3·75   £4·85

£3·94   £4·13

£2·73   £1·66

Calendars

1 Write the months of the year in order.

 December

 January

 July

 November

 March

 February

 April

 September

 May

 June

 October

 August

2 Which months have 30 days?

3 How many months have 31 days?

4 When is the next year when there will be 29 days in February?

 Look at this month's calendar. Which days are there five of? How many Saturdays next month? Make up some questions for your partner to answer.

Calendars

List the months in each season.

Write the months of the year in order.

1

December   August   November   September   May

April   June   October   January   February   July   March

WINTER   SPRING   SUMMER   AUTUMN

Look at Chang's calendar for June, then answer the questions.

Monday	Tuesday	Wednesday	Thursday	Friday	Saturday	Sunday
1	2	3	4	5	6	7
8	9	10	11	12	13	14

On what date did Chang go:

2   swimming   3   camping   4   to Aunt Su's house

5   horse riding   6   to his trumpet lesson   7   to band practice?

Draw a calendar for what you will do this week.

Calendars

Study Jim's calendar, then answer the questions.

Monday	Tuesday	Wednesday	Thursday	Friday	Saturday	Sunday
1 Washing day	2	3 Dad to go back to Navy	4	5	6 Aunt May for lunch	7
8 Washing day	9	10	11	12 Rally at town hall	13	14 Aunt May for lunch
15 Washing day	16 Post Gran's present	17	18	19 Gran's birthday	20	21
22 Washing day	23	24 Help with harvest	25 Help with harvest	26 Help with harvest	27 Help with harvest	28 Harvest festival
29 Washing day	30					

1 How many Tuesdays were there?

2 Which were the washing days?

3 On which date did Dad return to the Navy?

4 How many days was Jim helping with the harvest?

5 How many times did Aunt May come to lunch? What were the dates?

6 How long between posting Gran's present and her birthday?

7 When was the rally?

Talk with a partner about how your month's calendar might be different.

Calendars

1 Solomon Grunday was born on Monday 3rd June. On what day of the week was he exactly 1 month old? What was the date of the first Sunday in his life?

2 If Christmas Day (25th December) is a Saturday, on what day is New Year's Eve? What is the date of the first Saturday in the New Year? On what day does 1st February fall?

3 Mary-Jane had her 10th birthday on the 11th day of the 11th month. It was a Wednesday. On what day of the week will she be 10 years and 1 month old?

 **Explore**

You will need a monthly calendar for this year.

Which day of the week occurs most often in the year?

On what day of the week would a year need to start to have as many Saturdays as possible?

Which months have the same numbering of days, for example, Monday 1st, Tuesday 2nd, etc?

How many full weekends (Saturday and Sunday) are there in the year?

How many months in the year start on a Monday? Would this be the same for every year?

Carroll diagrams

Creepy Crawly Caterpillar
Climbing up my tent
Creepy Crawly Caterpillar
I think it's time you went

	Begins with 'c'	Does not begin with 'c'
Ends with 'y'	creepy	my
Does not end with 'y'	caterpillar	up it's

Which other words from the poem go in the:

1 yellow box   2 blue box   3 pink box   4 green box?

Where would we write the words:

5 clammy   6 cat   7 box   8 try?

9 Suggest two of your own words to go in each box.

Carroll and Venn diagrams

1   Copy the Carroll diagram and write the numbers in the correct spaces.

75
20
65
48
84
50

	50 or more	Not 50 or more
Digit total is 12 or more		
Digit total is not 12 or more		

40
62
97
49
39
17
81

2   Copy the Venn diagram. Write the numbers in the correct spaces.

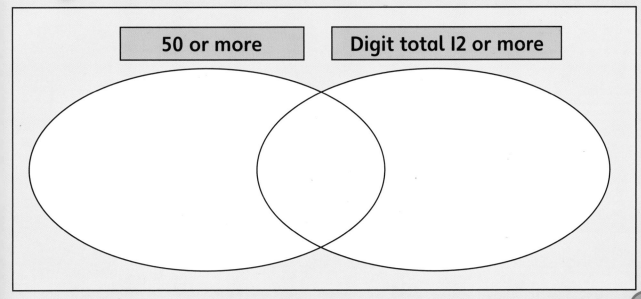

| 50 or more | Digit total 12 or more |

Carroll and Venn diagrams

Vehicles, colours, animals, birds
Elephants, fish, insects and words
Now we can sort them the way they fit best
Neatly and tidily, into two sets.

Columns and rows
Arranged on my pages
Ready and waiting
Receiving in stages
Old and new objects
Like jellies or jam
Letting me sort them.

Carroll diagrams

Choose either a Venn or Carroll diagram to sort the words in the poems.

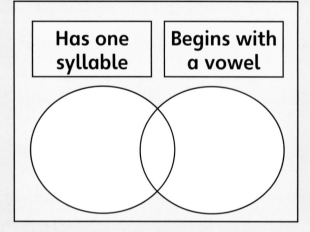

	Has one syllable	Has ~~one syllable~~
Begins with a vowel		
Begins with a ~~vowel~~		

Work with a partner. Can you decide the criteria used to produce this Carroll diagram? Add some more words of your own.

	Car Cup Dog Mouse *Tin Plate Cat*	*Big Red Soft Blue* *Hard Sad*
	Motorbike Giraffe *Hamster Needle* *Window Sofa Chimney*	*Purple Happy Little* *Orange Gentle*